Walking the Thames

A Complete Guide to England's Longest and Most Famous River

Monalisa Scott

Table of contents

INTRODUCTION

Welcome to Walking the Thames

Introducing "Walking the Thames: A Guide to England's Iconic River," the essential travel companion for discovering one of the most cherished natural beauties in all of England. We cordially encourage you to go off on a voyage of discovery along the scenic banks of the River Thames, from its source in the Cotswolds to its magnificent finish at the Thames Barrier, with the help of this all-inclusive travel guide.

Find the Thames's True Nature

Millions of people have a particular place in their hearts for the River Thames, which is a representation of the natural beauty, rich history, and cultural legacy of England. It has shaped the towns and landscapes along its banks for ages as a vital conduit for commerce, travel, and leisure.

Your Handbook for Memorable Experiences

"Walking the Thames" is the key to discovering the delights of this famous river, regardless of your level of experience hiking, interest in history, or simple love of the outdoors. Our book provides thorough route descriptions, insider insights, and useful suggestions to help you make the most of your trip across Thames, from serene rural routes to busy metropolitan promenades.

"Walking the Thames" is your go-to guide for appreciating the splendor and grandeur of England's famous river, whether you're planning a leisurely walk, a multi-day hike, or a picturesque river cruise. Put on your walking shoes, gather your spirit of adventure, and get ready for an amazing trip down the Thames River.

Let's get started exploring the Thames!

About This Guide

With this all-inclusive travel guide, you'll need no other companion as you set off on a trip along the magnificent Thames River. This book is intended to help you get the most out of your visit to one of England's most famous rivers, regardless of your level of expertise with hiking, wildlife, or history.

What to anticipate
Everything you need to organize and have a fantastic walking trip along the Thames is included in this book. We can help you every step of the way, from helpful advice and suggested routes to fascinating insights into the river's rich history, cultural importance, and scenic beauty. This tour has plenty to offer everyone, whether your preference is for leisurely walks through scenic countryside or urban exploration in vibrant riverbank cities.

Important characteristics
The Thames Path is a National Trail that traces the river's path from its source in the Cotswolds to the famous Thames Barrier and beyond. See detailed route descriptions here. With details on distance, topography, areas of interest, and suggested stops along the route, each part is meticulously documented.

Insider Advice & Suggestions: To make the most of your trip to Thames, take use of insider information and local understanding. Our professional suggestions will help you make the most of your trip, from hidden jewels and off-the-beaten-path attractions to the finest places to dine and stay.

Historical and Cultural Insights: Discover the rich cultural legacy and history of the Thames, from historic sites and medieval towns to current activities and attractions. Learn more about the importance of the river as a source of business, inspiration, and leisure throughout the ages.

Practical Information: To guarantee a hassle-free and pleasurable journey, gather vital information on food and lodging alternatives, safety advice, and transit choices. We have everything you need to be knowledgeable and ready, whether you're planning a multi-day expedition or a day walk.

Why Take a Thames Walk?
A unique chance to see England's varied landscapes, energetic towns, and centuries-old legacy at your own speed is provided by walking the Thames. The Thames offers something for everyone, whether your preference is for the thrill of big cities or peace and quiet in the beautiful countryside. By starting this voyage, you'll make lifelong memories in addition to taking in the splendor and grandeur of one of England's most famous rivers.

Allow this book to be your reliable travel companion as you set off on your Thames journey, offering motivation, direction, and useful counsel at every turn. "Walking the Thames: A Guide to England's Iconic River" is your key to discovering the beauties of this fabled river, regardless of previous travel experience. So prepare to experience the enchantment of the Thames River by putting on your boots, packing your spirit of adventure, and getting set. Your voyage is about to begin!

Tips for Walking the Thames

Walking the length of the Thames is an exciting excursion that offers amazing views, a wealth of historical information, and life-changing events.

Take into account some important pointers and suggestions to make the most of your stroll along the Thames:

Prior to embarking, allocate some time to meticulously map out your itinerary along the Thames Path. Think about how far you want to go each day, the sights you want to see along the route, and the facilities offered at each location. Use maps and guidebooks to get familiar with the route so you don't get lost and can maximize your time.

Examine the Weather: Before beginning your stroll, be sure to check the forecast since the weather by the Thames may be erratic. Bring rain gear, UV protection, and sturdy shoes, along with other clothes and equipment suitable for any situation. Remember that after rain, routes might become muddy or slick, so be careful and modify your speed appropriately.

Keep Yourself Hydrated and Energised: Strolling down the Thames may be strenuous on your body, particularly on hot and muggy days. Carry plenty of water with you, and fill up your bottle at approved water fountains and public restrooms along the way to stay hydrated. To maintain your energy levels throughout the day, pack foods that will help you stay energized, such energy bars, almonds, and dried fruit.

Take Rest Periods: While strolling down the Thames, pace yourself and pay attention to your body. Take frequent pauses to relax, drink some water, and take in the view. Before carrying on with your adventure, look for places with shade, seats, and picnic spaces where you may unwind and refresh. If you start to feel overwhelmed or tired, don't be afraid to abbreviate your walking days or change your schedule.

Respect the Natural Environment and Wildlife: The Thames is home to a wide variety of plants and animals, so make sure to show them some love while you're out and about. Steer clear of feeding animals, upsetting nesting birds, and leaving behind trash or food leftovers that might endanger local species. Adherence to signs and legislation aimed at safeguarding delicate environments is crucial. Please stick to authorized routes.

Interact with Locals: Getting to know the people living along the Thames and learning about their villages is one of the best things about walking the river. Spend some time chatting with locals, business owners, and other walkers you come across. They could provide insightful advice, suggestions, and anecdotes that improve your visit and strengthen your bond with the Thames.

Take Pictures: Carry a camera or smartphone to record your Thames stroll memories. Capture images of breathtaking scenery, important historical sites, and special moments to keep a record of your travels and show your loved ones. To keep track of your ideas, observations, and experiences throughout the journey, think about starting a blog or diary.

You will be well-prepared to set off on an amazing tour down the Thames and fully immerse yourself in the beauty, history, and culture of England's most famous river if you heed these advice and suggestions. So prepare to go on a walking tour of the Thames's treasures by putting on your walking shoes and packing a spirit of adventure.

PART I

PLANNING YOUR JOURNEY

Understanding the Thames: History, Geography, and Culture

Traveling down the famous Thames River is an amazing experience that offers exploration, adventure, and a better knowledge of the rich history, geography, and culture of England. It's important to learn about the importance of the Thames and the variety of landscapes it passes through before beginning your stroll along it.

Thames History: A River of Time
For millennia, the Thames River has been crucial in forming the history and character of England. The Thames has seen a great deal of action over the years,

from its modest origins as a little brook in the Cotswold Hills to its development into an essential river for commerce and transportation.

The Thames has historically been London's lifeblood, giving it access to the sea and enabling commerce with far-off places. Kings and queens, artists and authors, merchants and fisherman have all called its banks home, leaving their imprints on the river's illustrious history.

Thames Geography: From Source to Sea

The Thames flows through a variety of landscapes across its 200-mile course, from busy towns and attractive villages to rolling hills and meandering farmland. For the purpose of organizing your Thames walk and enjoying the breathtaking scenery and natural beauties that await you along the route, it is essential that you comprehend the river's topography.

The trip starts at the source of the Thames, a little spring that feeds the river in the Cotswold Hills. After then, it meanders through peaceful countryside, passing past quaint towns like Windsor, Oxford, and Henley-on-Thames, before arriving at the vibrant city of London. The Thames eventually empties into the huge English Channel at sea, where its waters blend together.

Culture Along the Thames: An Interwoven Web of Customs.

Discover the rich tapestry of historical monuments, landmarks, and cultural institutions that line the banks of the Thames, a place steeped in history and tradition.

Explore a multitude of cultural experiences along the Thames, from world-class museums and art galleries to historic sites and ancient castles.

You may experience the local way of life and friendliness at thriving markets, small tea houses, and riverside pubs that you'll come across on your travels. Enjoying authentic English cuisine, going to a riverbank celebration, or taking in famous sites like Windsor Castle or the Tower of London are just a few ways to engage with England's rich cultural legacy along the Thames.

You will have a greater appreciation for this famous river and its significance in forming England's past and present if you are aware of its geography, history, and culture. Equipped with this understanding, you're prepared to set off on an amazing voyage down the Thames, where every turn of the river holds the possibility of fresh discoveries and life-changing events.

Best Time to Walk the Thames

Choosing the right time to set off on your Thames cruise is essential to making the most of your comfort and pleasure. The Thames Path walking experience is influenced by a variety of factors, including seasonal events, river conditions, and weather.

1. Spring (March to May): As nature emerges from its winter hibernation and the countryside blossoms, spring is a great time to stroll along the Thames. Most of the time, the weather is pleasant, with temperatures rising gradually and extended daylight hours making for better strolling. In addition, springtime along the Thames Path means less tourists, which makes it simpler to take in the peace and beauty of the river and its environs.

2. Summer (June to August): Summertime in England is the busiest time of year for tourists along the Thames, as many come to take advantage of the long, sunny days and beautiful weather. With pleasant weather and plenty of sunlight, the summer months are great for strolling, but you should be ready for more people and more expensive lodging. You may escape the midday heat and the busiest periods on the trail by scheduling your stroll for later in the evening or early in the morning.

3. Autumn (September to November): With the trees along the riverbanks changing into a kaleidoscope of vivid hues, autumn is a lovely season to stroll down the Thames. Early in the season, the weather is still pleasant for strolling, and the combination of the clear sky and golden tones makes for a stunning scene as you go. Autumn also brings with it the chance to take part in seasonal activities and festivities along the Thames, such riverbank celebrations and harvest fairs.

4. Winter (December to February): With fewer daylight hours, lower temperatures, and the potential for bad weather, winter may be a difficult season to stroll the Thames. Winter, however, may also be a magnificent time to see the river in a new light for those who are courageous enough to face the weather. The festive mood in the towns and villages along the river may give an added layer of pleasure to your trip, and the calmer and more meditative stroll along the Thames Path in the winter months is another benefit.

In the end, the ideal time to take a stroll along the Thames is determined by your own interests and priorities. Travelers visiting England's famed river will find that each season provides its own distinct pleasures and difficulties, whether you like the brilliant hues of fall, the warmth of summer, or the serenity of winter. Through careful consideration of weather, crowds, and seasonal events, you can choose the ideal moment to start your Thames trip and make lifelong memories.

Choosing Your Route: From Source to Sea

For hikers who want to discover England's most famous river, there are several alternatives available along the Thames Path. If a shorter stretch of the path better fits your interests and physical capabilities, you may choose to walk it all the way from the source in the Cotswolds to the sea at the Thames Barrier. Additionally, you may choose to stroll on the north or south side of the river, or use boats and bridges to cross between the two.

It's a wonderful task to walk the full path from source to sea, which will take you through a variety of landscapes, rich history, and lively culture. The river will transform from a little brook in the countryside to a powerful river running through the center of London. You will go through several charming villages, peaceful water meadows, and ancient towns and cities. Windsor Castle, Hampton Court Palace, Oxford, Henley-on-Thames, Reading, Marlow, Runnymede, Kew Gardens, Westminster, Tower Bridge, Greenwich, and the Thames Barrier are just a few of the well-known sites and attractions that you may come across along the Thames. The path length is 185 miles (298 km), and depending on your speed and amount of sightseeing time, you may finish the path in two to three weeks.

You may choose a desirable stretch of the route for a shorter stroll if you would like. There are many possibilities, from a few kilometers to a few days, to suit a variety of preferences and skills. The official Thames Path website has maps and comprehensive information for each stretch.

Among the most well-liked portions are:

The Thames emerges from a field near Kemble and grows into a stream as it runs through the Cotswolds. This is the first leg of the path, The Source to Cricklade. Along the route, you'll stop at a few quaint towns and stroll through serene farmland, woods, and marshes. It is possible to do the 12 miles (19 km) in one or two days.

- **Oxford to Abingdon**: This portion passes through Oxford's historic center, where you may take in the renowned colleges, cathedrals, and museums as well as the vibrant atmosphere of the college town. After that, you'll follow the river as it meanders through the countryside, passing by some magnificent mansions and historic bridges. At the conclusion of your journey is Abingdon, one of the oldest towns in England with a picturesque riverbank and a rich history. It is possible to complete 10 miles (16 km) in one or two days.

- **Henley-on-Thames to Marlow**: This stretch of the path, which hugs the river known for its rowing and regattas, is among its most picturesque and pleasurable sections. The starting point for your journey is Henley-on-Thames, a bustling town including a stunning historic core and a museum devoted to the sport of rowing. After there, you'll follow the river as it meanders through the Chiltern Hills, passing past some well designed homes and gardens as well as several charming locks and islands. Your journey will conclude at Marlow, a quaint hamlet with a beautiful suspension bridge and literary ties to Mary Shelley and Jerome K. Jerome. It is possible to complete the 9 miles (14 km) in one or two days.

- Windsor to Hampton Court: You will stroll by two of the most renowned and majestic palaces in England as you traverse some of the most regal and historic sections of the Thames. Your journey begins at Windsor, where you may explore the Queen's house and the oldest and biggest inhabited castle on Earth, Windsor Castle. After that, you will follow the river as it passes by many charming towns and villages, including Eton, Datchet, Runnymede, and Staines, as well as the picturesque Windsor Great Park. Your journey will conclude in Hampton Court, where you can take in the breathtaking gardens and maze of Hampton Court Palace, which formerly served as the residence of Henry VIII and his many wives.

The 22-mile (35-kilometer) course may be completed in two or three days, or it can be broken up into shorter segments.

Westminster to Greenwich: This route takes you through the center of London, passing by some of the most recognizable and well-known sites and landmarks along the Thames. Beginning in Westminster, you will get the opportunity to see Big Ben, the Houses of Parliament, and Westminster Abbey.

Next, you will follow the Thames as it flows by some of the most striking and significant structures in the city, including the Shakespeare's Globe, the London Eye, the Tate Modern, the Tower of London, and the Tower

Bridge. After arriving at Greenwich, you may explore the Cutty Sark, the Royal Observatory, and Greenwich Park. It is possible to complete the 9 miles (14 km) in one or two days.

Greenwich to the Thames Barrier: This trail's last stretch allows you to watch the Thames come to a stop at the ocean. You will begin in Greenwich, where you may take in the town's rich maritime history and culture. After there, you will follow the river as it passes through the Docklands, an area that was once a commercial and industrial center but is now a bustling, contemporary quarter. The Thames Barrier, an amazing technical achievement that keeps London safe from floods, is where you will finish up. It is possible to complete the 7 miles (11 km) in one or two days.

You will have to select which side of the river to travel, whether you want to walk the whole path or just a portion of it. The Thames Path is mostly straightforward to follow and well indicated, however there are a few places where you'll need to use ferries or bridges to cross the river, or when the path splits into two different routes on each side. The official Thames Path website has maps and information for each part.

The following are a few variables that might affect your bank preference:

- The attractions and scenery: On some parts of the path, one bank may provide more fascinating or picturesque vistas and sights than the other. You could choose to stroll on the south bank, for instance, to view more of the historical and cultural sites, such the Shakespeare's Globe, the Tate Modern, and the Cutty Sark, on the stretch from Westminster to Greenwich. However, if you would rather stroll along the north bank, you may view more of the area's natural and regal beauties, including Hampton Court Palace, Runnymede, and Windsor Great Park, on the stretch from Windsor to Hampton Court.

- Accessibility and amenities: On one side of the path, there may be fewer or more access points, lodging options, public transportation, food and drink, and restrooms than on the other. For instance, the south bank, which has more towns and villages like Sandford, Nuneham Courtenay, and Culham, may provide more alternatives and convenience on the stretch from Oxford to Abingdon. On the other side, the north bank, which has more towns and villages including Hambleden, Hurley, and Bisham, may offer you greater convenience and alternatives along the stretch from Henley-on-the-Thames to Marlow.

- The length and difficulty: There may be more or less challenging parts of the path on one side of the river than the other, including hills, gates, stiles, and road crossings. For instance, the south side of the river, where the trail follows the river more closely, may have more obstructions and elevation variations than the north bank, where the trail follows a more straight path. This is especially true for the portion from the Source to Cricklade. However, the path runs through the

Docklands on the north bank, where there may be more obstructions and elevation variations than on the south bank, where the trail follows the river more closely. This is especially true for the portion from Greenwich to the Thames Barrier.

The final decision on which bank to choose is yours and your own. There's always the option to stroll both sides and compare them, or use bridges and boats to get between them. The most crucial thing is to appreciate the surroundings and the individuals you come across while taking in the river and stroll.

Packing Essentials: What to Bring on Your Thames Walk

Traveling the Thames Path is a unique way to see England's famous river, its breathtaking scenery, and its charming villages, all while fostering connections with nature, history, and culture. It is crucial to pack sensibly and be ready for the many weather conditions you may face on your journey in order to guarantee a pleasant and pleasurable trip.

The following is a list of things you should definitely pack for your Thames walk:

1. Comfortable Footwear: To tackle the various terrain of the Thames Path, you'll need a solid pair of hiking boots or walking shoes with strong ankle support. For extended walking days, choose well-cushioned, waterproof, and broken-in shoes to avoid blisters and pain.

2. Weather-appropriate Clothes: Pack layers that are simple to add or remove as required to be ready for erratic weather. Choose clothes that will wick away moisture to stay dry and comfortable even if it rains. Remember to include necessities like sunglasses, a hat or cap for sun protection, and a lightweight rain jacket.

3. Navigational Aids: Although much of the Thames Path is well signposted and simple to follow, it's always a good idea to pack a comprehensive map or guidebook to aid with route planning and navigation. For extra peace of mind, think about getting a portable GPS gadget or downloading a dependable navigation app on your smartphone.

4. Hydration and Snacks: Pack a reusable water bottle and an ample supply of snacks, such as trail mix, energy bars, and fresh fruit, to ensure you are well-hydrated and well-fueled for your adventure. If you want to refill your water bottle from natural water sources along the journey, think about bringing along a lightweight portable water filter device or purification tablets.

5. First Aid Kit: Keep a small first aid kit with basic supplies like adhesive bandages, antiseptic wipes, painkillers, blister pads, and any personal prescriptions you may require on hand to be ready for minor cuts and maladies. Including a basic survival pack with supplies like a multi-tool, emergency blanket, and whistle is also a smart idea.

6. Sun Protection: Use sunscreen with a high SPF rating and reapply it often throughout the day to shield yourself from the sun's damaging rays. To prevent sunburn on your face and neck, remember to include lip balm with SPF protection and a lightweight, breathable sun hat.

7. Personal needs: Don't forget to bring personal goods like a lightweight towel, hand sanitizer or wet wipes, a camera or smartphone to record memories, and any necessary personal hygiene products. A small backpack or daypack may also be used to carry your needs.

Packing these must-have goods and being ready for the many weather conditions you can experience along the Thames Path will ensure that you're ready for an amazing and pleasurable trip down England's most famous river. So prepare to discover the history and beauty of the Thames like never before by putting on your walking shoes and grabbing your bag.

PART II

EXPLORING THE THAMES PATH

Thames Path Overview: Highlights and Must-See Attractions

Traveling the Thames Path is an enthralling experience that lets visitors fully appreciate the splendor, legacy, and customs of England's most famous river. From its start in the Cotswolds to the Thames Barrier in London, the 184-mile Thames Path presents a varied mosaic of environments, points of interest, and adventures just waiting to be discovered.

1. Source to Lechlade: Start your Thames excursion at the charming Cotswold hamlet of Kemble, where the river originates. On approach to Lechlade, follow the meandering waterways as they pass through picturesque towns and important historical sites. The peaceful meadows of Cricklade and the historic market town of Lechlade, where you may take in the stunning St. John's Lock and Bridge, are highlights of this stretch.

2. Lechlade to Oxford: Continue your journey from Lechlade to Oxford, a historic city well-known for its esteemed university and breathtaking architecture. Walking the Thames Path offers you the chance to see beautiful meadows, charming riverfront towns, and bucolic rural areas. You may also stop along the route to see important historical sites like Kelmscott Manor and Buscot Park.

3. Oxford to Wallingford: The Thames Path travels south from Oxford's busy downtown, providing beautiful views of the river and the surrounding landscape. The lovely village of Wallingford, where you may tour the remains of Wallingford Castle and wander along the riverside promenade, and the quaint town of Abingdon, with its ancient market square and medieval architecture, are highlights of this stretch.

4. Wallingford to Reading: The Thames Path offers a variety of scenic natural areas and urban settings as you go. Head toward the energetic metropolis of Reading via scenic riverside parks, busy market towns, and tranquil rural areas. The little hamlet of Pangbourne, with its quaint riverbank bars and gorgeous walks along the Thames, is one of this section's highlights.

5. Reading to Windsor: The Thames Path meanders from the vibrant metropolis of Reading through gorgeous rural areas and quaint riverbank towns before arriving at the ancient town of Windsor. The picturesque towns of Cookham and Bray, with their storied taverns and quaint riverbank promenades, and the magnificent Windsor Castle, one of the Queen's royal homes, are highlights of this region.

6. Windsor to Hampton Court: Follow the Thames Path as it meanders through Berkshire and Surrey's lovely countryside to continue your trip. The ancient town of Maidenhead, with its famous railway bridge over the river, and the magnificence of Hampton Court Palace, one of England's most spectacular royal houses, are highlights of this stretch.

7. Hampton Court to Putney Bridge: The Thames Path winds through the lush suburbs of south west London, providing picturesque vistas of the river and its famous sites. It begins with the imposing magnificence of Hampton Court Palace. Highlights of this area include the renowned Putney Bridge, a historic monument across the river, and the lovely riverside towns of Teddington and Richmond, with their quaint taverns and attractive parks.

8. Putney Bridge to Tower Bridge: The Thames Path winds through the center of London, providing expansive vistas of the city's famous structures and skyline. This section's highlights include the fashionable stores and cafés along the streets of Chelsea and Battersea, as well as the ancient sites of Westminster and Tower Bridge, which provide stunning views of the river and the surrounding city.

9. Tower Bridge to the Thames Barrier: The last section of the Thames Path winds through East London's energetic communities, where contemporary construction meets old sites. Highlights of this part include the magnificent Thames Barrier, an engineering wonder that keeps London safe from floods, the ancient Canary Wharf docks, and the famous O2 Arena.

A voyage of discovery, the Thames Path provides an enthralling look into the natural beauty, history, and culture of England's most famous river. The Thames Path offers something for every kind of tourist, whether it is beautiful hikes through stunning countryside, ancient sites rich in heritage, or energetic metropolitan environments teeming with activity. So grab your spirit of adventure, lace on your walking shoes, and set off on a once-in-a-lifetime trip down one of the most famous rivers in the world.

Section 1

Source to Lechlade

From the river's source in the Cotswolds to the town of Lechlade, where the Thames becomes boat-navigable, is where this stretch of the Thames Path leads. Along the journey, you will see the river transform from a trickle to a stream, take in the picturesque rural surroundings of the Cotswold Water Park, and stop at a few quaint towns and ancient churches.

The source of the Thames is located in a secluded field close to Kemble hamlet; it is identified with an inscribed stone. The riverbed is dry in the spring and mostly dry in the summer for most of the year. The Thames Head Inn, a bar that prides itself on being the first on the Thames, or the adjacent Kemble train station are two good starting points for walks.

Following the young river as it flows through meadows and forests and over a few small roads and bridges, you may track it from its source. Ewen is the first settlement you come to. A mill and a pond are seen there. The next settlement is called Somerford Keynes, and it has a church, a bar, and a store. This is where you enter the Cotswold Water Park, a region formed by the excavation of gravel that has over 140 lakes. While some of the lakes are set aside for wildlife and conservation, others are utilized for recreational and water sports purposes. Along with a range of creatures including otters, deer, and badgers, you may observe a variety of birds like swans, geese, ducks, herons, and kingfishers.

The Thames Path passes by several lakes and marshes as it meanders through the water park. You may either follow the main path or take various side trips to explore the park. You will come to the end of the right of upstream navigation as you approach the town of Cricklade, which is the first notable community on the Thames. With a strong Saxon heritage, Cricklade is home to a beautiful medieval church, a museum, and a number of bars and stores. In late April, hundreds of rare snakeshead fritillaries bloom in the North Meadow, a nature reserve.

After leaving Cricklade, follow the river as it meanders through the rural areas, going past a few hamlets and farms. Using footbridges or stepping stones, you will cross the river many times while taking in the views of the hills and water meadows. You will arrive in the settlement of Castle Eaton, where a bar and a church from the twelfth century may be seen. At this point, the Thames Path briefly leaves the river and travels to Upper Inglesham via a footpath and bridleway.

Rejoining the river at Upper Inglesham, you continue it to Inglesham, where you may explore the church of St John the Baptist, a treasure of ancient architecture rebuilt by 19th-century poet and artisan William Morris. The Thames and Severn Canal enters the Thames here, and the River Coln exits it. The 18th-century canal, which connected the two rivers, is now overgrown and abandoned. The Round House, a toll house where the canal boats paid their tolls, is still visible.

You reach Lechlade, where the Thames becomes a significant river and the first boats arrive, on the last length of this segment. Lechlade is a bustling town with a range of facilities, including stores, cafés, bars, and lodging. A few sites are located nearby, including the St. Lawrence Church from the fifteenth century, the Halfpenny Bridge, a beautiful stone bridge with seventeen arches, and the Trout Inn, a riverfront bar where author Shelley penned a poem. Lechlade is a well-liked location for boating and fishing, as well as the beginning point of several boat excursions and cruises on the Thames.

Section 2

Lechlade to Oxford

This stretch of the Thames Path connects the city of Oxford, which is home to the oldest university in the English-speaking world, with the village of Lechlade, where the Thames becomes a significant river. You will see several ancient towns and villages along the route, take in the pastoral beauty of the Vale of White Horse, and see the river transform from a stream to a navigable canal.

Lechlade is a bustling town with a range of facilities, including stores, cafés, bars, and lodging. A few sites are located nearby, including the St. Lawrence Church from the fifteenth century, the Halfpenny Bridge, a beautiful stone bridge with seventeen arches, and the Trout Inn, a riverfront bar where author Shelley penned a poem. Lechlade is a well-liked location for boating and fishing, as well as the beginning point of several boat excursions and cruises on the Thames.

Following the river through the countryside from Lechlade, you will pass past a few farms and hamlets. Once you get to the hamlet of Radcot, you will be able to view the Radcot Bridge, which dates back to the 12th century and is the oldest bridge on the Thames. The Thames Path briefly leaves the river here and travels along a road and a track to the settlement of Tadpole Bridge, where there is a campground and a tavern.

Rejoining the river at Tadpole Bridge, you continue it to the town of Bampton, where you can see the church of St Mary, with a Saxon font and a Norman tower. Another well-known use of Bampton is as the setting for the made-up hamlet of Downton in the hit television program Downton Abbey. Some of the locations from the episode, including the tavern, church, and library, are visible.

After leaving Bampton, follow the river as it meanders through the Vale of White Horse, so called because of a big chalk image of a horse perched on a hill. You'll go past several charming villages along the way, such Northmoor, Shifford, and Chimney, where you may discover manor homes, taverns, and churches. A medieval stone bridge with fifteen arches may be seen at Newbridge, where you will also cross the River Windrush, a tributary of the Thames.

The town you come to next is Abingdon, which has been inhabited continuously since the Iron Age and is the oldest town in England. There are many attractions in Abingdon, including a market, a park, a theater, and a museum. The Abbey, an ancient Benedictine monastery established in the seventh century and disbanded by Henry VIII in the sixteenth, is another place you may see. The checker hall, the long gallery, and the gatehouse are among the structures that still stand from the Abbey.

Following the river through the countryside from Abingdon passes via a few settlements and islands. You will arrive in Sandford-on-Thames hamlet, where you will view the biggest and deepest lock on the Thames, the Sandford Lock, and the Sandford Lasher, a weir that forms a rapid and is a well-liked kayaking location. There's a boat, a hotel, and a tavern here.

This section's last stretch leads you to Oxford, the city of dreaming spires and the location of the oldest institution in the English-speaking world, the institution of Oxford. Oxford is a dynamic, multicultural city with a strong intellectual and cultural legacy. Explore the university's several colleges, museums, libraries, and cathedrals. You may also take advantage of the stores, cafés, pubs, and theaters that serve both students and non-students. A few river-related attractions are also available, including the Folly Bridge, a stone bridge with a tower that served as the inspiration for Lewis Carroll's Alice in Wonderland, Christ Church Meadow, a picturesque park by the river, and the Oxford Botanic Garden, which is the oldest botanic garden in Britain.

You will need to select which side of the river to walk, whether you intend to walk the whole route or just a portion of it. The Thames Path is mostly straightforward to follow and well indicated, however there are a few places where you'll need to use ferries or bridges to cross the river, or when the path splits into two different routes on each side. The official Thames Path website has maps and information for every stretch, along with a free nautical chart that illustrates the river's characteristics. The Thames Path app is another option; it offers GPS tracking, offline maps, and walking-related information.

The following are a few variables that might affect your bank preference:

- **The attractions and scenery:** On some parts of the path, one bank may provide more fascinating or picturesque vistas and sights than the other. For instance, you could choose to stroll along the south bank, where you can view more of the villages and scenery, such as Radley, Kennington, and Iffley, on the stretch from Abingdon to Oxford. However, you could choose to stroll on the north bank along the stretch from Lechlade to Bampton, where you'll be able to view more of the river and the islands, such as Eaton Hastings, Rushey, and Buscot.

- **Accessibility and amenities:** On one side of the path, there may be fewer or more access points, lodging options, public transportation, food and drink, and restrooms than on the other. For instance, the north bank of the Thames, which has more towns and villages like Iffley, Kennington, and Sandford, may provide greater convenience and alternatives for travelers traveling from Oxford to Sandford-on-Thames. On the other side, the south bank, which has more towns and villages including Buckland, Longworth, and Appleton, may provide you more alternatives and convenience on the stretch from Bampton to Abingdon.

- **The length and difficulty**: There may be more or less challenging parts of the path on one side of the river than the other, including hills, gates, stiles, and road crossings. For instance, on the south bank of the Lechlade to Radcot segment, where the trail follows the river more closely, you can come across more obstacles and elevation variations than on the north bank, where the trail follows a more straight path.

However, the south bank, where the path goes through some urban areas, may have more barriers and elevation variations than the north bank, where the trail follows the river more closely. This is especially true for the portion from Sandford-on-Thames to Oxford.

The final decision on which bank to choose is yours and your own. There's always the option to stroll both sides and compare them, or use bridges and boats to get between them. The most crucial thing is to appreciate the surroundings and the individuals you come across while taking in the river and stroll.

Section 3

Oxford to Wallingford

This stretch of the Thames Path connects Wallingford, a medieval market town with a castle and museum, to Oxford, the site of the oldest university in the English-speaking world. You will see several charming towns and taverns along the route, take in the bucolic Oxfordshire countryside, and see the river transform from a passable stream into a broad, deep river.

Oxford is a dynamic, multicultural city with a strong intellectual and cultural legacy. You may take advantage of the shops, cafés, pubs, and theaters that serve both students and non-students, or you can tour the several colleges, museums, libraries, and cathedrals that comprise the University of Oxford. A few river-related attractions are also available, including the Folly Bridge, a stone bridge with a tower that served as the inspiration for Lewis Carroll's Alice in Wonderland, Christ Church Meadow, a picturesque park by the river, and the Oxford Botanic Garden, which is the oldest botanic garden in Britain.

Following the river through the countryside from Oxford will take you past a few farms and small towns. You will arrive at the hamlet of Iffley, where you may explore the Norman church with an amazing carved gateway and the lovely Iffley Lock with a wooden footbridge. There's a boat, a hotel, and a tavern here.

Proceed on the south side and cross the river at Iffley via the Iffley Lock footbridge. Some settlements and islands will pass by, such Sandford-on-Thames, where you can see the biggest and deepest lock on the Thames, the Sandford Lock, and the Sandford Lasher, a weir that generates a rapid and is a well-liked kayaking location. There's a boat, a hotel, and a tavern here.

The town you come to next is Abingdon, which has been inhabited continuously since the Iron Age and is the oldest town in England. There are many attractions in Abingdon, including a market, a park, a theater, and a museum. The Abbey, an ancient Benedictine monastery established in the seventh century and disbanded by Henry VIII in the sixteenth, is another place you may see. The checker hall, the long gallery, and the gatehouse are among the structures that still stand from the Abbey.

Following the river as it meanders through the countryside from Abingdon, you will pass past a few farms and hamlets. You will arrive at the hamlet of Culham, where you will witness the five-arched, ancient Culham Bridge as well as the Culham Lock, a lock with a brick bridge and a lock keeper's cabin. There's a campground and a bar here.

Proceed on the north side and cross the river at Culham via the Culham Bridge. Some settlements and islands will pass by, such Clifton Hampden, where you can view the Sir George Gilbert Scott-designed Clifton Hampden Bridge made of wood, and the Barley Mow, a bar that was mentioned in Jerome K. Jerome's Three Men in a Boat. This area has a ferry, a church, and a store.

This leg ends at Wallingford, a picturesque market town complete with a museum and a castle. With a rich past that extends back to the Saxon era, Wallingford was once a mint and a royal fortress. You may see the Wallingford Museum, which showcases the town's history and archeology, as well as the Wallingford Castle, a destroyed fortress that Oliver Cromwell besieged during the Civil War. The Wallingford Market Place, a sizable area including a town hall and a monument of Wallingford-born jurist and judge William Blackstone, is another attraction.

You will need to select which side of the river to walk, whether you intend to walk the whole route or just a portion of it. The Thames Path is mostly straightforward to follow and well indicated, however there are a few places where you'll need to use ferries or bridges to cross the river, or when the path splits into two different routes on each side. The official Thames Path website has maps and information for every part.

The following are a few variables that might affect your bank preference:

- **The attractions and scenery**: On some parts of the path, one bank may provide more fascinating or picturesque vistas and sights than the other. For example, you could choose to stroll along the north bank on the stretch from Oxford to Iffley, where you will be able to view more of the city and university, including the Magdalen College, the Folly Bridge, and the Christ Church Meadow.

However, you could want to walk down the south bank where you can view more of the landscape and the villages, such Long Wittenham, Little Wittenham, and Dorchester-on-Thames, on the stretch from Culham to Wallingford.

- **Accessibility and amenities**: On one side of the path, there may be fewer or more access points, lodging options, public transportation, food and drink, and restrooms than on the other. For instance, the south bank, which has more towns and villages like Sandford-on-Thames, Radley, and Kennington, may provide more alternatives and convenience on the stretch from Iffley to Abingdon. On the other side, the north bank, which has more towns and villages including Sutton Courtenay, Appleford, and Didcot, may provide you more alternatives and convenience on the stretch from Abingdon to Culham.

- **The length and difficulty**: There may be more or less challenging parts of the path on one side of the river than the other, including hills, gates, stiles, and road crossings. For example, the route goes through many urban neighborhoods, including Benson, Cholsey, and Moulsford, on the north bank. This portion, from Wallingford to Culham, may have additional difficulties and elevation variations. However, the path runs through many rural districts, like Burcot, Clifton Hampden, and

Nuneham Courtenay, on the south bank, where you may experience additional challenges and elevation variations on the portion from Culham to Oxford.

The final decision on which bank to choose is yours and your own. There's always the option to stroll both sides and compare them, or use bridges and boats to get between them. The most crucial thing is to appreciate the surroundings and the individuals you come across while taking in the river and stroll.

Section 4

Wallingford to Reading

This stretch of the Thames Path connects the energetic metropolis of Reading with the medieval market town of Wallingford, offering a wide range of cultural and recreational opportunities. Along the route, you will see the river change from a broad, deep river to a crowded, urban canal, take in the rural splendor of the Chiltern Hills, and stop at several quaint towns and pubs.

Wallingford is a medieval market town including a museum and a castle. With a rich past that extends back to the Saxon era, Wallingford was once a mint and a royal fortress. You may see the Wallingford Museum, which showcases the town's history and archeology, as well as the Wallingford Castle, a destroyed fortress that Oliver Cromwell besieged during the Civil War. The Wallingford Market Place, a sizable area including a town hall and a monument of Wallingford-born jurist and judge William Blackstone, is another attraction.

Following the river through the rural area from Wallingford, you will see a few farms and hamlets. As you approach the community of Moulsford, you will see the Moulsford Railway Bridge, a brick structure built by renowned Victorian engineer Isambard Kingdom Brunel to span the Thames for his Great Western Railway. A hotel and a tavern are located here.

Proceed along the south side of the river after crossing it at Moulsford via the Moulsford Railway Bridge. You will sail by a few villages and islands, including South Stoke, where you can visit the Perch and Pike, a 17th-century tavern and inn, and the South Stoke Church, a 13th-century church with a wooden bell tower. A store and a ferry are located here.

The next town you come to is Goring-on-Thames, home of the five-arched stone Goring Bridge, which links Goring to Streatley-on-Thames, its twin town. Numerous facilities, including stores, cafés, bars, and hotels, are located here. The Goring Lock, a lock with a wooden footbridge and a lock keeper's house, and the Goring Church, a 12th-century church with a Norman tower and an Edward Burne-Jones stained glass window, are both worth seeing.

You follow the river as it meanders through the very beautiful Chiltern Hills from Goring-on-the-Thames. You will pass by several charming places, such Lower

Basildon, where you can visit the Beale Park, a wildlife park with a lake and a train, and the Basildon Park, a Palladian palace with parkland and a garden. A tavern, hotel, and ferry may be found in Pangbourne, where you can also cross the River Pang, a tributary of the Thames.

This section's last stretch leads you to Reading, a thriving city with a wide range of cultural and recreational opportunities. With a long history that dates back to the Roman era, Reading is a significant center for commerce and transportation. The Reading Abbey, a medieval Benedictine monastery established in the twelfth century and disbanded by Henry VIII in the sixteenth, is open for exploration. The remnants of the abbey's structures, including the mill, the hospital, and the entrance, are visible. You may also go to the Forbury Gardens, a public park including a lion statue and a fountain, and the Reading Museum, a museum showcasing the town's history and artistic creations.

You will need to select which side of the river to walk, whether you intend to walk the whole route or just a portion of it. The Thames Path is mostly straightforward to follow and well indicated, however there are a few places where you'll need to use ferries or bridges to cross the river, or when the path splits into two different routes on each side. The official Thames Path website has maps and information for every part. You may also use a free nautical chart to see the river and its characteristics.
The following are a few variables that might affect your bank preference:

- The attractions and scenery: On some parts of the path, one bank may provide more fascinating or picturesque vistas and sights than the other. For example, you could opt to stroll on the north bank where you can view more of the river and the islands, including Cleeve, Littlestoke, and Cholsey, on the portion from Wallingford to Moulsford. However, you could choose to walk on the south bank where you can view more of the countryside and the villages, such Streatley-on-Thames, Lower Basildon, and Whitchurch-on-Thames, on the stretch from Goring-on-Thames to Pangbourne.

- Accessibility and amenities: On one side of the path, there may be fewer or more access points, lodging options, public transportation, food and drink options, and restrooms than on the other. For instance, you could find greater convenience and alternatives on the south bank of the Thames, where there are more towns and villages, such as South Stoke, Cleeve, and Streatley-on-Thames, on the stretch that runs from Moulsford to Goring-on-Thames. On the other side, the north bank, which has more towns and villages including Purley-on-Thames, Tilehurst, and Caversham, may provide you more alternatives and convenience on the stretch from Pangbourne to Reading.

- The length and difficulty: There may be more or less challenging parts of the path on one side of the river than the other, including hills, gates, stiles, and road crossings. In the instance of the Wallingford to Moulsford portion, the south bank presents a greater number of barriers and elevation changes due to the trail's closer alignment with the river, whilst the north bank offers a more direct approach. However, the path runs through some woody sections on the north bank, where there may be more barriers and elevation changes than on the south bank, where the track follows the river more closely. This is especially true for the portion from Goring-on-Thames to Pangbourne.

The final decision on which bank to choose is yours and your own. There's always the option to stroll both sides and compare them, or use bridges and boats to get between them. The most crucial thing is to appreciate the surroundings and the individuals you come across while taking in the river and stroll.

Section 5

Reading to Windsor

You will encounter a gorgeous section of the river as you go along the Thames Path, which meanders from the ancient town of Reading to the magnificent town of Windsor. This stretch of the route gives hikers an immersive experience that highlights the varied landscapes and rich history of the Thames Valley by combining stunning natural beauty with interesting historical sites and quaint riverbank villages.

Synopsis
Around 22 miles (35 kilometers) of the Thames Path go from Reading to Windsor, offering hikers a beautiful scenery of winding riverbanks, verdant meadows, and

peaceful forests. En route, you'll see picturesque towns, riverbank bars, and famous sites like Windsor Castle, one of the official palaces of the British monarchy, and the ancient town of Henley-on-Thames.

Standouts

Caversham Lock: Start your adventure in Reading, a thriving city with a long history of industry. Take the riverside route from Caversham Lock, which meanders through lovely parks and green areas with breathtaking views of the river and surrounding countryside.

Pass through the enchanting hamlet of Sonning-on-Thames, which is well-known for its old watermill, riverbank gardens, and cute houses. Wander along the riverbank or have a leisurely lunch at one of the quaint pubs or riverfront cafés in the hamlet.

Reach the well-known town of Henley-on-Thames, which is well-known for its yearly Royal Regatta and charming riverbank location. Wander around the town's old streets, pay a visit to the River & Rowing Museum, or just unwind by the river and observe the passing scenery.

Marlow: Proceed to the lively town of Marlow, where you'll discover a quaint blend of local stores, riverfront restaurants, and classic pubs. Admire the expansive views of the river and the surrounding countryside as you cross the famous Marlow Bridge.

Windsor: Finish your stroll at the charming medieval town of Windsor, which is the site of the world's oldest and biggest inhabited castle, Windsor Castle. To round up your Thames Path exploration, take a boat ride on the river, explore the castle grounds, or take a walk down the Long Walk.

Realistic Aspects to Take into Account
Walking distance and time: Depending on your speed and preferences, the 22-mile (35-kilometer) walk from Reading to Windsor may be completed in one to two days. Before leaving, be sure to check the tidal schedule and the weather prediction and adjust your route as necessary.

Lodging & eating: The route is along with a variety of lodging and eating choices, from quaint bed and breakfasts to riverbank cafés and gastropubs. be reservations for your lodging well in advance, particularly during the busiest times of the year. While you're there, be sure to experience the local food and friendliness.

transit: Accessing the beginning and ending sites of your walk is simple since Reading and Windsor have excellent public transit connections. Windsor may be reached by bus from surrounding towns and cities or by rail from London Waterloo. Regular train services operate between London Paddington and Reading.

A fascinating excursion that highlights the natural beauty, historical sites, and quaint communities of the

Thames Valley is walking the Thames Path from Reading to Windsor. This stretch of the route provides a unique experience that encapsulates the spirit of England's famous river, whether you're an experienced walker or just taking a casual stroll. So grab your camera, tie up your walking shoes, and get ready to enjoy the Thames's natural beauty on foot.

Section 6

Windsor to Hampton Court

Overview of the Route

The route begins at Windsor, the location of the famous Windsor Castle, and meanders down the placid waters of the Thames, passing past quaint riverfront settlements, lush vegetation, and gorgeous farmland. There are many different types of attractions to be found along the way, such as majestic houses and historic sites, cozy taverns, and riverfront cafés.

Standouts

Start your tour at Windsor, where you may visit the world's oldest and biggest inhabited castle, the spectacular Windsor Castle. Admire the State Apartments' magnificence, meander around the lovely grounds, and engage in the daily, time-honored custom of the Changing of the Guard ceremony.

Eton College: One of the most famous and esteemed private institutions in the world, Eton College is located just over the river from Windsor. Enjoy a leisurely walk around Eton's historic town, which is home to the famous College Chapel, quaint shops, and cafés.

Runnymede: Proceeding down the Thames, you will traverse the ancient meadow of Runnymede, where King John signed the Magna Carta in 1215. Examine the monuments and memorials honoring this significant occasion as you ponder this turning point in English history.

Your adventure comes to an end at Hampton Court Palace, a stunning Tudor mansion encircled by lovely grounds and rich in history. Admire the grandeur of the Great Hall and Chapel Royal, meander through the well-known labyrinth, and explore the luxurious State Apartments.

Useful Advice
Distance: Depending on your route of choice and any diversions you may take, the estimated distance from Windsor to Hampton Court.

Duration: Allocate a whole day to explore this stretch of the Thames Path, giving yourself enough time to stop at points of interest and take in the breathtaking scenery as you go.

Facilities: This section of the Thames Path has an abundance of amenities, including cafés, pubs, and bathrooms, to guarantee that you have all you need for a relaxing and pleasurable stroll.

Beginning at Windsor Castle and ending at Hampton Court Palace, Section 6 of the Thames Path provides an enthralling tour through natural beauty, history, and culture. This stretch of the Thames Path is likely to fascinate and please, whether you're a history buff, a wildlife lover, or just looking for a picturesque stroll along England's famed river. So grab your camera, tie up your walking shoes, and get ready for an amazing journey down the Thames River.

Section 7

Hampton Court to Putney Bridge

This portion of the Thames Path leads to the bustling Putney Bridge, the starting point of the annual Oxford and Cambridge Boat Race, from the majestic Hampton Court Palace, the former residence of Henry VIII and his many wives. You will see several ancient villages and parks along the route, take in the urban panorama of southwest London, and see the river transform from a rural, regal stream to a contemporary, metropolitan one.

With a 16th-century history, Hampton Court Palace is one of the most striking and well-liked sites on the Thames. You may take in the architecture, artwork, and furnishings as well as tour the castle and its breathtaking grounds. A few of the elements that depict the life and era of Henry VIII and his court are also visible, including the Hampton Court Maze, the Tudor Kitchens, the Chapel Royal, and the Great Hall. Additionally, there are some facilities including stores, cafés, and restrooms.

You may follow the river from Hampton Court Palace through the London suburbs, via a few cities and islands. Once you arrive at the town of Kingston upon Thames, you will be able to view the 19th-century Kingston Bridge, a stone structure with five arches. Numerous facilities are available here, including stores, bars, eateries, and lodging. Additionally, you may see the Kingston Museum, which showcases the town's history and artwork, and the Kingston Church, a 12th-century church with a spire and a coronation stone.

Following the river as it meanders through the countryside from Kingston upon Thames, you will pass past a few villages and parks. After passing through the settlement of Teddington, you will come across the Teddington Lock, a set of three locks and a weir that marks the end of the Thames's tidal portion. There's a ferry, a café, and a tavern here.

Proceed on the south side and cross the river at Teddington via the pedestrian Teddington Lock footbridge. You will pass by a few towns and islands, including Ham, where you may see the Marble Hill House, a Palladian house with a park and a view of the river, and the Ham House, a 17th-century mansion with a garden and several paintings. Additionally, you will cross the tributary of the Thames, the River Crane, in Twickenham, where there is a ferry, a hotel, and a tavern.

The Richmond Bridge, an 18th-century stone bridge with five arches, is seen in Richmond, the next town you come to. Numerous facilities, including stores, cafés, bars, and hotels, are located here. You may also go to Richmond Hill, a hill with a terrace and a well-known view of the Thames, and Richmond Park, a sizable royal park with a deer park and a view of the London skyline.

You follow the river from Richmond through the London suburbs, via a few towns and islands. You will arrive at the town of Kew, where you can view the 19th-century Kew Bridge, a stone bridge with three arches. There's a boat, a hotel, and a tavern here. Additionally, there is the Kew Palace, a former royal mansion with a museum and lawn, and the Kew Gardens, a botanical garden with a variety of plants, trees, and glasshouses.

The last portion of this segment leads to Putney, where you can view the 19th-century Putney Bridge, a stone structure with five arches. Numerous facilities are available here, including stores, bars, eateries, and lodging. Additionally, you may explore the Putney Church, a 15th-century building including a tower and a stained glass window, as well as the Putney Pier, a pier where you can go on a Thames boat ride or cruise. The yearly Oxford and Cambridge Boat Race, a rowing competition between the two universities that draws thousands of spectators, also begins at Putney.

You will need to select which side of the river to walk, whether you intend to walk the whole route or just a portion of it. The Thames Path is mostly straightforward to follow and well indicated, however there are a few places where you'll need to use ferries or bridges to cross the river, or when the path splits into two different routes on each side. The official Thames Path website has maps and information for every part. You may also use a free nautical chart to see the river and its characteristics.

The following are a few variables that might affect your bank preference:

- **The attractions and scenery**: On some parts of the path, one bank may provide more fascinating or picturesque vistas and sights than the other. For example, you could want to stroll on the north bank of the Thames where you can view more of the river and the islands, such Eel Pie Island, Raven's Ait, and Thames Ditton, on the stretch from Hampton Court Palace to Kingston upon Thames. However, if you want to view more of the countryside and parks like Syon Park, Brentford, and Barnes, you may choose to stroll on the south bank along the stretch that runs from Kew to Putney.

- **Accessibility and amenities**: On one side of the path, there may be fewer or more access points, lodging options, public transportation, food and drink, and restrooms than on the other. For instance, the south bank, which has more cities and villages including Surbiton, Thames Ditton, and Hampton Wick, may provide greater convenience and alternatives for travelers traveling from Kingston upon Thames to Teddington. On the other side, the north bank, which has more towns and villages including Twickenham, St Margarets, and Isleworth, may provide you greater convenience and alternatives on the stretch from Teddington to Richmond.

- **The length and difficulty:** There may be more or less challenging parts of the path on one side of the river than the other, including hills, gates, stiles, and road crossings. For instance, the trail may have more obstacles and elevation changes on the south bank when it passes through some urban areas, like Mortlake, Chiswick, and Strand-on-the-Green, on the Richmond to Kew section. Conversely, the north bank, where the trail passes through some rural areas, like Kew Green, Brentford, and Barnes, on the Kew to Putney section may have more obstacles and elevation changes.

The final decision on which bank to choose is yours and your own. There's always the option to stroll both sides and compare them, or use bridges and boats to get between them. The most crucial thing is to appreciate the surroundings and the individuals you come across while taking in the river and stroll.

Section 8

Putney Bridge to Tower Bridge

This stretch of the Thames Path connects you to the historic Tower Bridge, one of the most recognizable sights on the river, from the bustling Putney Bridge, the starting point of the annual Oxford and Cambridge Boat Race. You will see various historic and cultural sites along the route, take in the urban beauty of downtown London, and see the Thames transform from a contemporary, metropolitan canal to a historic, regal one.

Constructed in the 1800s, Putney Bridge is a five-arched stone bridge. It links Putney and Fulham, two neighborhoods rich in boating and rowing traditions. The annual Oxford and Cambridge Boat Race, a rowing competition between the two universities that draws thousands of spectators, begins in Putney. Numerous facilities are available, including stores, bars, eateries, and lodging. Additionally, you may explore the Putney Church, a 15th-century building including a tower and a stained glass window, as well as the Putney Pier, a pier where you can go on a Thames boat ride or cruise.

You may follow the river from Putney Bridge as it meanders through London's suburbs, passing by a few cities and islands. Once you get in the town of Hammersmith, you can view the 19th-century wrought iron-designed Hammersmith Bridge, a suspension bridge with two towers. Numerous facilities, including stores, cafés, bars, and hotels, are located here. Additionally, you can see the 17th-century Hammersmith Church, which has a fresco and a spire, as well as the Hammersmith Apollo, a music and entertainment center that performs comedies and concerts.

Proceed on the south side and cross the river in Hammersmith via the Hammersmith Bridge. There will be a few towns and parks along the route, such Barnes, where you can explore the Barnes Wetland Centre, a natural reserve with a lake and a range of birds and animals, and the Barnes Bridge, a 19th-century railroad bridge with two arches and a pedestrian walkway. Additionally, you will cross the tributary of the Thames, the River Wandle, in Wandsworth, where there is a hotel, a ferry, and a bar.

The next town you come to is Battersea, home of the 19th-century steel bridge known as the Battersea Bridge, which has five arches. Numerous facilities are available here, including stores, eateries, bars, and lodging. You may also explore the Battersea Power plant, a former coal-fired power plant that is being converted into a mixed-use complex, and Battersea Park, a sizable public park with a lake, a zoo, and a pagoda.

Following the river as it runs through the heart of London from Battersea, you will pass by some of the most recognizable and well-known buildings and landmarks along the Thames. After arriving at the town of Westminster, you will be able to observe the Westminster Bridge, a 19th-century stone bridge with seven arches. Numerous facilities, including stores, cafés, bars, and hotels, are located here. The Houses of Parliament, which house the British government and are home to Big Ben, the Westminster Abbey, a Gothic cathedral where the country's kings are crowned and interred, and the London Eye, a massive Ferris wheel that provides sweeping views of the city, are more attractions.

Proceed on the north bank after crossing the river at Westminster via the Westminster Bridge. Some of the most striking and significant structures in the city will be visible to you as you go by, including the Temple Church, a circular church constructed in the twelfth century by the Knights Templar, the Monument, a column honoring the Great Fire of London in 1666, and

Somerset House, a neoclassical building with a gallery and a fountain. At Blackfriars, you will also cross the River Fleet, an underground river that empties into the Thames and is home to a hotel, a ferry, and a tavern.

One of the most well-known sites on the Thames is Tower Bridge, which is reached at the end of this segment. Built in the 19th century, Tower Bridge is a bascule bridge with two towers and a promenade. It links Southwark with the City of London, two historically significant neighborhoods. Numerous facilities are available, including stores, eateries, bars, and lodging. In addition, there's the Tower Bridge Exhibition, a museum showcasing the bridge's history and workings, and the Tower of London, a medieval stronghold that served as a royal residence, a jail, and a treasury.

You will need to select which side of the river to walk, whether you intend to walk the whole route or just a portion of it. The Thames Path is mostly straightforward to follow and well indicated, however there are a few places where you'll need to use ferries or bridges to cross the river, or when the path splits into two different routes on each side. Visit the official Thames Path website for details and maps of each stretch, or use this free nautical chart to see the river and its highlights. The Thames Path app is another option; it offers GPS tracking, offline maps, and walking-related information.

The following are a few variables that might affect your bank preference:

- **The attractions and scenery**: On some parts of the path, one bank may provide more fascinating or picturesque vistas and sights than the other. For example, you could want to stroll on the south bank where you can view more of the river and the islands, including Fulham, Wandsworth, and Chiswick, on the stretch from Putney Bridge to Hammersmith. However, if you want to view more of the city and its attractions, such as Somerset House, Temple Church, and Monument, you may choose to stroll on the north bank along the stretch from Westminster to Tower Bridge.

- **Accessibility and amenities**: On one side of the path, there may be fewer or more access points, lodging options, public transportation, food and drink, and restrooms than on the other. For instance, the south bank, which has more towns and villages like Barnes, Putney, and Wandsworth, may provide greater convenience and alternatives along the Hammersmith to Battersea stretch. However, in the area between Battersea and Westminster, where there are more towns and villages like Chelsea, Pimlico, and Victoria, you could find greater convenience and alternatives on the north bank.

- **The length and difficulty:** There may be more or less challenging parts of the path on one side of the river than the other, including hills, gates, stiles, and road crossings. For instance, the path runs through many metropolitan districts, including the South Bank,

Waterloo, and Bankside, on the portion from Westminster to Blackfriars, where you may come across additional difficulties and elevation variations on the south bank. However, the path travels past some historic locations, like the Tower Hill, Fleet Street, and the City of London, on the north bank throughout the stretch from Blackfriars to Tower Bridge, where you may come across greater challenges and elevation variations.

The final decision on which bank to choose is yours and your own. There's always the option to stroll both sides and compare them, or use bridges and boats to get between them. The most crucial thing is to appreciate the surroundings and the individuals you come across while taking in the river and stroll.

Section 9

From Tower Bridge to the Thames Barrier

On the concluding leg of your Thames adventure, you will see an intriguing mix of new architecture, historic sites, and vibrant waterfront life. This stretch of the Thames Path provides an enthralling look into London's inventive approach to sustainable urban development and its historic maritime legacy.

1. The Tower of London and Tower Bridge:
Start your stroll at the famous Tower Bridge, a representation of the architectural magnificence and

technical brilliance of London. Take a moment to appreciate the exquisite details of this magnificent Victorian bridge, which has two towers that are instantly recognizable and tiny spans that open to let large ships pass through. Explore the ancient Tower of London, a UNESCO World Heritage Site surrounded by centuries of mystery, intrigue, and royal history, which is close by.

2. Docks at St. Katharine

If you follow the Thames Path east, you'll come upon St. Katharine Docks, which is a hidden treasure tucked away among the tall buildings of London's financial center. These charming docks, which were first constructed in the 19th century to handle cargo ships, have been turned into a bustling marina with stores, cafés, and restaurants. Sail or cruise the riverside promenade at your leisure and take in the sight of the opulent yachts and sailboats that now occupy St. Katharine Docks.

3. Dock at Canary Wharf

London's thriving financial center, Canary Wharf, greets you with a breathtaking vista of steel and glass buildings reaching far into the sky. Canary Wharf, home to banks, financial institutions, and international enterprises, is evidence of London's standing as a major player in the world economy. Pause to appreciate the striking design of structures like the UK's tallest skyscraper, One Canada Square.

4. The Thames Barrier

The stunning Thames Barrier, an engineering wonder and an essential part of London's flood defense system, is where your Thames voyage comes to an end. This massive, intimidating structure spans the width of the river and is made up of 10 giant steel gates that can be raised to safeguard the city from storm and tidal surges. Visit the visitor center to learn about the building and operation of the Thames Barrier, as well as its history and importance. Interactive exhibits and educational displays are available.

Take a minute to consider the amazing views and sensations you have seen so far as you approach the conclusion of Section 9. This part of the Thames Path provides an enthralling tour across London's past, present, and future, from the ancient sites of Tower Bridge and the Tower of London to the futuristic skyline of Canary Wharf and the technical wonder of the Thames Barrier. As you go on toward the ocean, be ready to be moved by the strength and beauty of England's most famous river.

Section 10

Thames Barrier to the Sea

When you travel the last section of the Thames, you will see the river change from a busy river to a magnificent tidal estuary that empties into the North Sea. This portion of the tour will take you on an amazing journey as you visit the last part of England's famous river, from the iconic Thames Barrier to the stunning landscapes of the Thames Estuary.

1. The Thames Barrier's discovery

The Thames Barrier, an engineering wonder at Woolwich Reach that spans the river, is a symbol of environmental preservation and technical skill. Discover the amazing engineering and history of this imposing building, which was constructed to shield London from floods and tidal waves.

2. Investigating Woolwich and Greenwich

You will travel through the ancient boroughs of Greenwich and Woolwich as you go downstream, where centuries' worth of maritime history are brought to life. Explore the maritime history of Woolwich Arsenal and the Thames Path Sculpture Trail, as well as the Royal Observatory and the Cutty Sark at Greenwich.

3.Third, Getting Around the Thames Estuary

You will approach the serene beauty of the Thames Estuary, where the river expands and the terrain significantly changes, leaving behind the urban panorama of London. Admire the enormous stretches of mudflats, salt marshes, and marshes that support a diverse range of animals, such as rare plant species, migrating birds, and seals.

4.Villages & Towns Along the Coast

You may get a taste of traditional marine life in the quaint coastal towns and villages that line the estuary.

Discover the ancient port towns of Sheerness and Gravesend, meander down Margate's and Southend-on-Sea's waterfront promenades, and eat fresh seafood in charming eateries by the sea.

5. The Last Mile

When you get close to the Thames mouth, you can see where the river and the sea converge, the estuary's waters meet the wide North Sea. Think back for a minute on your trip down England's most famous river, from its modest origins in the Cotswolds to its magnificent end at the sea.

From the barrier to the sea, walking the Thames is an amazing experience that provides unmatched chances to learn about the natural beauty, history, and culture of the river. This last leg of your Thames adventure promises to be a fitting end to your journey along one of England's most famous waterways, whether you're admiring the technological wonders of the Thames Barrier, touring the historic towns of Greenwich and Woolwich, or losing yourself in the peace of the Thames Estuary.

PART III

EXPLORING THAMES-SIDE TOWNS AND VILLAGES

Thames-side Towns and Villages: Hidden Gems and Local Treasures

Beginning your adventure down the Thames Path, you'll find that the river is not just a breathtaking natural feature, but also a point of entry to quaint communities full of character and rich in history. Every Thames-side village, from sleepy riverbank hamlets to vibrant market towns, has its own distinct mix of local gems that are just waiting to be discovered, as well as history and culture.

1. Richmond-upon-Thames: Located on the outskirts of London, this charming town is well-known for its gorgeous riverbank, lush gardens, and graceful Georgian architecture. Visit sites like Richmond Park, which is home to herds of deer and breathtaking panoramic views of the river, and explore the historic Richmond Green and the Thames Embankment.

2. Henley-on-Thames: Known for its yearly regatta and traditional English charm, Henley-on-Thames is a timeless city of refinement and elegance. Stroll through the quaint alleys of the town, which are adorned with Tudor-style houses; pursue upscale stores and galleries; and savor meals along the river with views of the famous Henley Bridge and racing course.

3. Marlow: Located in the center of the Thames Valley, Marlow is a thriving market town with a picturesque riverfront location and a strong literary tradition. Take a leisurely boat ride down the river, explore the town's ancient alleys, and pay a visit to the quaint Higginson Park—all while following in the footsteps of literary greats like Mary Shelley and Jerome K. Jerome.

4. Windsor: A royal riverfront town rich in royal history and architectural magnificence, Windsor is home to Windsor Castle, the oldest and biggest inhabited castle in the world. Take a leisurely boat ride down the Thames to take in the breathtaking views of the town's riverbank, explore the castle grounds, and meander through Windsor Old Town's charming alleyways.

5. Goring and Streatley: The twin settlements of Goring and Streatley, which are nestled at the base of the Chiltern Hills, provide a serene haven among breathtaking scenery. Explore old taverns and churches, take leisurely strolls along the river, and take in the tranquil ambiance of these charming settlements along the Thames.

6. Oxford: Known for both its famous spires and its esteemed university, Oxford is a city renowned for both its architectural beauty and intellectual brilliance. For a distinctive viewpoint of this ancient city, enjoy punting along the River Cherwell, explore the old colleges, and stroll through the lovely parks and gardens of the city.

A visit to the cities and villages along the Thames River is a must if you want to get a deeper understanding of England's rich history and make connections with the local way of life. Each village along the Thames has a unique history and treasures to uncover, making them must-visit locations on your Thames tour. From historic sites to undiscovered jewels. Thus, while you travel down England's famous river, take your time to visit these quaint towns and villages and let their distinct charm and character make a lasting impression.

Historical Landmarks and Architectural Marvels

A plethora of historical sites and architectural wonders that provide intriguing insights into England's rich past and cultural legacy may be found as you travel down the Thames. Every riverside monument, from historic mansions and castles to recognizable bridges and imposing cathedrals, tells a tale from ages gone by and permanently alters the surrounding terrain.

1. Windsor Castle: The oldest and biggest inhabited castle in the world, Windsor Castle stands magnificently on the banks of the Thames in the ancient town of Windsor. This majestic stronghold, which dates back more than 900 years, has served as the residence of

British kings for many centuries and is a symbol of the nation's royal past. Explore the luxurious State Apartments, take in the magnificence of St. George's Chapel, and watch the daily, centuries-old Changing of the Guard event.

2. Hampton Court Palace: One of England's most recognizable historical sites, Hampton Court Palace is a Tudor architectural marvel that is situated upstream from Windsor. Constructed by Cardinal Wolsey during the 16th century and subsequently enlarged by King Henry VIII, the palace has breathtaking gardens, elaborately designed royal chambers, and elaborate courtyards. Highlights include the Tudor kitchens, the Great Hall (formerly the site of opulent dinners hosted by Henry VIII), and the renowned labyrinth (the nation's oldest hedge labyrinth).

3. The Tower of London: One of the most famous monuments in the city, the Tower of London is located in the center of London on the north bank of the Thames and is recognized as a UNESCO World Heritage Site. Throughout its lengthy history, the tower, which William the Conqueror erected in the eleventh century, has functioned as a royal residence, a stronghold, and a jail. Explore the medieval White Tower, take in the splendor of the Crown Jewels in the Jewel House, and take a guided tour to discover the intriguing and sinister history of the tower.

4. Tower Bridge: A masterpiece of Victorian engineering, Tower Bridge is located next to the Tower of London and is a well-known emblem of London. This magnificent bridge was finished in 1894 and has towering towers with elaborate Gothic embellishments and a unique bascule design. In addition to seeing the amazing gears that power the bridge's functioning, visitors may descend into the Engine Rooms or stroll over the high-level decks for panoramic views of the city and Thames.

5. St. Paul's Cathedral: One of the most cherished monuments in the city, St. Paul's Cathedral is an architectural marvel that dominates the skyline of downtown London. Sir Christopher Wren created the cathedral's exquisite interior, which is filled with elaborate mosaics, sculptures, and stained glass windows. The cathedral has an impressive dome and a sophisticated façade. It was built in the late 17th century. To experience the spiritual importance of the cathedral, visitors may join a service or climb to the top of the dome for breathtaking views of the city.

6. Oxford University: One of the oldest and most esteemed colleges in the world is located in the ancient city of Oxford, which you will come across as you go upstream from London. Oxford University was established in the twelfth century and is made up of a magnificent array of colleges, libraries, and academic buildings that represent a wide range of historical architectural styles. The Bodleian Library, the Radcliffe Camera, and Christ Church College's recognizable spires are among the highlights.

Taking in the historical sites and architectural wonders along the Thames is like taking a trip down memory lane, providing an insight into England's rich cultural legacy and colorful history. Every landmark, from regal mansions and medieval castles to recognizable bridges and imposing cathedrals, has a distinct history and makes an effect on everyone who sees it. So put on your walking shoes, get ready to be mesmerized by the historical tapestry of the river, and set off on a voyage of exploration along the Thames.

PART IV

ENJOYING THAMES ACTIVITIES AND ATTRACTIONS

Outdoor Adventures and Recreational Opportunities Along the Thames

There are a plethora of outdoor activities and recreational possibilities available along the Thames River that suit all interests and levels of fitness. There's something for everyone along England's famous river, whether you're an adrenaline addict, a nature lover, or just want to relax in a beautiful setting.

1. Strolling and Mounting

Discovering the natural splendor of the river and its environs doesn't end with strolling along the Thames Path. The Thames Path, which has more than 180 miles of officially designated walking routes, provides many chances for leisurely strolls, strenuous excursions, and picturesque exploration. You will be rewarded with stunning vistas, quaint towns, and an abundance of animals along the way, regardless of whether you decide to walk the full route or just a portion of it.

2. Bike riding and cycling

The Thames provides a network of bike-friendly routes and cycling trails that meander through scenic countryside and along riverbanks for those who would rather explore on two wheels. Cycling enthusiasts may take pleasure in leisurely rides through serene towns, thrilling off-road routes, or strenuous long-distance routes offering a distinctive viewpoint of the Thames and its environs.

3. Kayaking & Boating

Water sports fans can find lots of chances for boating, kayaking, and canoeing on the Thames River. Take a tour of the river at your own speed by renting a kayak or paddleboard, and enjoy the picturesque splendor of the surrounding area as you make your way through peaceful waters and secret coves. An alternative is to take a boat trip or river cruise, which offers guided excursions that highlight historical sites, natural ecosystems, and cultural attractions while offering a unique viewpoint of the Thames.

4. Angler & Fishing

The Thames River is a well-liked location for fishermen and fishing lovers due to its well-known diversified and prolific fish population. Enjoy the peace and quiet of the river's banks while casting your line and trying your luck at catching a variety of freshwater species, such as trout, salmon, perch, and pike. Regardless of your level of experience, the Thames provides plenty of chances for a leisurely day of fishing in breathtaking settings.

5. Observing Wildlife and Birds

For birdwatchers and nature lovers, the Thames River and the marshes that surround it provide vital habitats for a diverse range of bird species, making it a sanctuary. Take your binoculars and travel to one of the numerous bird sanctuaries and nature reserves along the river to see a variety of birds, such as swans, ducks, kingfishers, and herons. Observe various fauna, including seals, otters, and sometimes even deer, as you discover the scenic attractions of the Thames.

There is no limit to the outdoor adventures and enjoyment that the Thames River has to offer, from exciting water sports and animal encounters to relaxing walks and picturesque bike rides. Whatever your preference, England's famous river offers thrilling experiences as well as peaceful times for contemplation. Put on your hiking boots, get your paddle, and get ready to take in the breathtaking scenery and thrilling action of the Thames.

Thames Cruises and Riverboat Tours

While experiencing England's famous river from the deck of a cruise ship or riverboat trip gives a distinct and immersive experience, walking the Thames Path offers a different viewpoint. There are many ways to explore the history, beauty, and charm of the River Thames while taking advantage of the conveniences of a boat, from relaxing sightseeing cruises to exhilarating speed boat experiences. We will explore the world of riverboat excursions and Thames cruises in this part of "Walking the Thames: A Guide to England's Iconic River," outlining the many choices and experiences they provide.

1. Relaxed Tours of the Sights
Sedentary sightseeing cruises down the Thames are a great choice for anyone looking for a laid-back and picturesque experience. Usually leaving from the heart of London, these excursions meander along the river, taking in famous sites including Tower Bridge, the Houses of Parliament, and the Tower of London. In addition to enjoying the expansive vistas, passengers may relax and enjoy the educational commentary on the historical background and cultural value of the locations along the route.

2. Cultural and Historical Tours

Guided riverboat trips that highlight the rich legacy and cultural sites of the Thames are essential for history fans and culture vultures. These trips often include pauses at historic locations where guests may disembark and walk about before resuming the journey, such as Hampton Court Palace, Greenwich, and the Royal Naval College. The importance of the monuments that line the river's banks and the part the river played in forming London's history are both fascinatingly revealed by knowledgeable guides.

3. Dinner Cruises and Entertainment in the Evenings

Dinner cruises and other nighttime entertainment choices provide a special fusion of eating, dancing, and sightseeing against the background of London's lit skyline, making for an unforgettable night out. These cruises provide an amazing experience, whether you're commemorating a particular event or just want to spend a romantic evening on the river. Savor fine dining, enjoy beverages on the deck, and dance the night away as you sail by famous sites illuminated by dusk.

4. Exciting Speed Boat Experiences

High-speed speedboat excursions down the Thames provide an exciting opportunity for thrill-seekers and adrenaline addicts to explore the river. Feel the wind in your hair as you drive past well-known locations at top speed. Then, hang on tight as your expert captain makes daring bends and twists. These speedboat excursions provide an adrenaline-pumping experience unlike anything other, with lively music playing and a spirit of adventure in the air.

Riverboat excursions and Thames cruises provide a wide variety of experiences to suit every interest and desire, giving visitors the chance to see England's most famous river from a different angle. Every tourist may choose a Thames cruise experience that suits them, whether they want an exciting speedboat adventure, a romantic dinner cruise, a guided historical tour, or a leisurely sightseeing cruise. Thus, get on board, set sail, and be ready to be mesmerized by the splendor and grandeur of the Thames River.

Museums, Galleries, and Cultural Attractions

As you walk along the banks of the Thames, you'll encounter a wealth of museums, galleries, and cultural attractions that offer fascinating insights into England's rich history, art, and heritage. From world-renowned institutions to hidden gems tucked away in riverside towns and villages, these cultural destinations provide a diverse array of experiences that will enrich your journey along the iconic river.

1. Tate Modern (London)

Located on the south bank of the Thames near the Millennium Bridge, the Tate Modern is one of the world's leading contemporary art museums. Housed in a converted power station, the museum showcases an impressive collection of modern and contemporary art, including works by Picasso, Warhol, and Hockney. Don't miss the stunning views of the river and city skyline from the museum's rooftop terrace.

2. British Museum (London)
Situated in the heart of London, the British Museum is a treasure trove of world history and culture. Its vast collection spans over two million years of human history, featuring artifacts from ancient civilizations around the globe. Highlights include the Rosetta Stone, the Elgin Marbles, and the Egyptian mummies.

3. Hampton Court Palace (Richmond upon Thames)
Step back in time at Hampton Court Palace, a magnificent Tudor palace located on the banks of the Thames in Richmond upon Thames. Explore the opulent state apartments, stroll through the lush gardens, and immerse yourself in the palace's rich history, which dates back to the reign of King Henry VIII.

4. Windsor Castle (Windsor)
Perched atop a hill overlooking the Thames, Windsor Castle is the oldest and largest inhabited castle in the world. Explore the State Apartments, St. George's Chapel, and the Queen Mary's Dolls' House, which showcases exquisite miniature interiors. Don't miss the Changing of the Guard ceremony, a quintessentially British tradition that takes place within the castle grounds.

5. River and Rowing Museum (Henley-on-Thames)
Located in the picturesque town of Henley-on-Thames, the River and Rowing Museum celebrates the history and heritage of rowing, rivers, and the natural world. Discover fascinating exhibits on the sport of rowing, the wildlife of the Thames, and the literary legacy of local author Kenneth Grahame, who wrote "The Wind in the Willows."

6. Chiswick House and Gardens (Chiswick)
Escape the hustle and bustle of London and explore the tranquil beauty of Chiswick House and Gardens. Designed by the renowned landscape architect Capability Brown, the gardens feature lush green lawns, ornamental ponds, and classical temples. Visit the Palladian villa, which houses a fine collection of art and furnishings, and enjoy a leisurely stroll along the riverfront promenade.

From world-class art museums and historic palaces to charming local galleries and cultural institutions, the Thames is lined with an array of museums, galleries, and cultural attractions that offer something for every interest and taste. Whether you're a history buff, art enthusiast, or nature lover, these cultural destinations provide captivating experiences that will enrich your journey along England's iconic river. So take the time to explore these cultural treasures and discover the stories and heritage of the Thames.

PART V

DINING AND ACCOMMODATIONS ALONG THE THAMES

Culinary Delights and Local Eateries

Discovering the charming banks of the Thames is a culinary adventure as well as an aesthetic pleasure. Travelers may find a wide variety of eating establishments along the famous river that highlight the greatest of British cuisine and other delicacies. Dining along the Thames provides a gastronomic adventure that excites and satisfies every palette, from sophisticated restaurants providing gourmet delights to quaint riverfront pubs serving basic pub grub.

Gourmet Treats Along the Thames

A mouthwatering variety of gastronomic treats awaits you along the Thames Path, ready to tantalize your palate. At a quaint riverbank café, begin your day with a substantial English breakfast. Here, you can indulge in classic dishes like bacon, eggs, sausages, and baked beans, all served with freshly made tea or coffee. Visit a quaint pub by the river for lunch and tuck into traditional British fare like plowman's lunch, shepherd's pie, and fish and chips, all of which are perfectly paired with a cool pint of local ale or cider.

When night comes, treat yourself to a wonderful meal at one of the classy restaurants in the Thames, where chefs with flair highlight the best seasonal ingredients and creative cooking methods. The Thames provides a wide variety of eating alternatives to suit every taste and occasion, from contemporary gastropubs and riverfront bistros to fine dining restaurants with Michelin-starred cuisine.

Local Restaurants Near the Thames
The Thames is lined with little neighborhood restaurants and hidden treasures that provide delectable cuisine in a laid-back atmosphere for those looking for a more informal eating experience. Indulge in handcrafted ice cream from a riverbank gelateria while taking in the picturesque surroundings, or stop by a charming tearoom for a classic cream tea, replete with scones, clotted cream, and jam.

Savor a diverse range of foods along the Thames, ranging from gourmet burgers and fresh seafood to exotic curries and meals with Mediterranean influences. Don't miss this chance to indulge in local delicacies and foreign cuisines. As you tour the riverfront towns and villages along the Thames, you'll find plenty of alternatives to satiate your gastronomic needs, whether you're in the mood for bold tastes or hearty classics.

Lodging Along the Thames: Cozy Inns and Riverside Retreats
Following a day of sightseeing along the Thames, retire to one of the numerous quaint lodging options that line

the banks of the river; these establishments provide tired tourists with cozy comfort and gracious hospitality. There are a variety of lodging options to fit every taste and budget, from contemporary hotels and luxury resorts to charming boutique bed & breakfasts and historic riverbank inns.

Staying at a charming inn or guest house will allow you to fully experience the beauty and character of the cities and villages along the Thames, where you can take advantage of individualized service and cozy lodging in a lovely environment. Riverbank hotels and resorts provide expensive services including spas, fine cuisine, and breathtaking views of the Thames for visitors looking for luxury and pleasure.

The Thames provides an array of lodging options to cater to all types of travelers, whether they are seeking a solitary exploration, a family-oriented vacation, or a romantic escape. Awaken to the tranquil sounds of the river, have a leisurely breakfast while taking in the view, and get ready for another exciting day of exploring England's most famous river.

Eating and sleeping by England's most famous river, the Thames, promises a unique experience that accentuates its beauty and charm. As they explore the stunning banks and ancient villages of the Thames, visitors may immerse themselves in the rich tradition and hospitality of the area, from indulging in gastronomic pleasures at riverfront cafés to relaxing in warm lodgings with magnificent views. As you travel down this famous river, prepare to enjoy the hospitality and tastes of the Thames. Bring an appetite and a spirit of adventure.

Accommodations Along the Thames: Hotels, Inns, and Bed & Breakfasts

The lodging options along the Thames provide something for every taste and budget, from boutique inns and historic hotels to charming bed & breakfasts, offering a cozy and welcoming spot to unwind and refresh after a day of exploring.

1. Historic lodging establishments
Staying at one of the Thames's historic hotels will allow you to fully experience the area's rich history and classic elegance. These opulent properties provide exquisite service, sumptuous lodging, and breathtaking river views. Historic hotels along the Thames provide a unique chance to savor the elegance and charm of bygone periods while taking advantage of contemporary conveniences and comforts, whether they are located in a former manor house, country estate, or riverbank palace.

2. Designer Hotels
Boutique inns along the Thames provide a warm and inviting setting for those looking for a more customized and private stay. Stylish décor, cozy lodging, and attentive service are common features of these little places, guaranteeing visitors a wonderful stay. For those looking for solitude and leisure among the splendor of the Thames, boutique inns are the ideal hideaway, hidden

away in serene rural surroundings or nestled in charming towns.

3. Breakfasts & Beds

Staying in a traditional bed and breakfast will let you experience the warmth and hospitality of the Thames, too. These family-run businesses provide visitors a home-away-from-home experience with their warm, comfortable lodging, freshly prepared breakfasts, and attentive service. Be it in charming cottages, old townhouses, or rural farmhouses, bed & breakfasts along the Thames provide a special chance to interact with the hosts and experience the genuine beauty of the river's environs.

4. Retreats by the Riverside

Riverbank retreats along the Thames provide a tranquil and dreamy haven from the rush of city life for individuals who would rather be closer to nature. With a variety of eco-friendly hotels, glamping spots, and comfortable cabins and cottages, these remote lodging options let visitors rediscover the river's and its surrounds' natural beauty. A peaceful haven where you may relax and rejuvenate among the tranquility of the Thames, riverbank retreats are ideal for romantic getaways, family vacations, or solitary explorations.

The lodging options along the Thames meet the requirements and tastes of any kind of tourist, whether they are looking for opulence and extravagance, charm and personality, or peace and quiet. These lodging options, which range from charming bed & breakfasts and riverfront getaways to historic hotels and boutique inns, provide the ideal starting point for seeing England's famous river and making lifelong memories along the way. Prepare to be amazed by the beauty and friendliness of this fabled river by packing your luggage and selecting your favorite getaway along the Thames.

PART VI

PRACTICAL INFORMATION

Transportation Options:Getting to and from the Thames

Knowing how to travel to and from the river's many access locations throughout its meandering course is the first step in exploring the famous Thames River. Whether you're going on a day excursion down the river or a multi-day expedition, knowing your alternatives for transportation will help your vacation go more smoothly and enjoyably. This is a thorough guide on the many ways to travel to and from the Thames:

1. **Train**: Taking the train is one of the easiest and most effective methods to get to the Thames. Major towns and cities along the river are easily accessible thanks to England's vast rail network, with terminals ideally situated close to the Thames Path. Regular trains go from London to places like Windsor, Reading, and Oxford, making it simple for visitors to get to the beginning of a Thames stroll. Check train timetables and purchase tickets well in advance, particularly during periods of high travel demand.

2. **Bus**: Another practical way to go to the Thames and see its many portions is via bus. Local bus services link the towns and villages along the river and run across the

Thames Valley area. It's also simple to get to the Thames from farther away with coach services from big towns like London that provide direct links to well-liked spots along the river. Bus stations are usually accessible by foot from the Thames Path, making it easy to switch between walking routes and public transit.

3. Car: Hiring a private automobile or renting one might be a great way for those who value flexibility in their travel plans to see the Thames. The Thames Path and its environs are easily explored because of major highways and roads that connect to cities and parking lots along the river. Remember that parking may be scarce in certain places, particularly at well-known tourist attractions, so it's best to research your alternatives in advance and look for a spot before you leave.

4. Bike: Riding a bike is a well-liked and environmentally responsible method to see the Thames and its beautiful surroundings. Bicycle-friendly pathways and designated cycling lanes make it safe and pleasurable to ride a bicycle along a large portion of the Thames Path. Towns along the river provide bike rentals, making it simple for visitors to access the Thames Path and go at their own speed. When cycling along the Thames, make sure you abide by the rules regarding road safety and cycling in the area.

5. Riverboat and Ferry: Taking a riverboat or ferry ride is a fun and picturesque way to see the Thames. Along the Thames, riverboat services are available for leisurely cruises and tourist trips that give expansive views of the river and its historical sites. Furthermore, ferry services provide quick passage across the river at several locations, making it simple for visitors to visit both banks of the Thames and take in its sights.

You can plan your trip to and from the Thames and make the most of your study of England's famous river by becoming acquainted with these transit alternatives. The Thames is waiting to amaze you with its beauty, history, and natural majesty, regardless of how you choose to get there, by rail, bus, vehicle, bicycle, or boat.

Safety Tips and Emergency Contacts

Safety should always be your first concern when you go out on the Thames Path. The river has possible risks that visitors should be aware of even if it also provides amazing sights and unforgettable experiences. While you tour England's famous river, bear in mind the following important safety advice and emergency numbers:

1. Keep Up with Information
Learn about the current weather and any possible dangers along the way, such as construction zones or flooded regions, before you go on your stroll. To guarantee a secure and pleasurable visit, keep up on local news and warnings.
2. Make a Route Plan:

Select a route based on your expertise and degree of fitness, taking accessibility, terrain, and distance into account. To prevent fatigue or injury, be honest with yourself about your limitations and pace yourself appropriately.

3. Wear the Right Clothes
Put on supportive, long-distance walking shoes that are comfortable, and layer your clothing to account for changing weather. To shield yourself from the weather, wear a hat, sunscreen, and a waterproof jacket. You should also think about bringing a first aid bag with the necessities.

4. Continue to Eat and Drink Well
Bring plenty of water and food so you can remain hydrated and focused while out for a stroll. Drink plenty of water to prevent dehydration, particularly on hot days. If needed, top up electrolytes with sports drinks or electrolyte pills.

5. Pay Attention to Your Environment
Always be on the lookout and mindful of your surroundings, particularly while traversing uneven terrain or strolling close to busy roadways. Be mindful of potential dangers such uneven terrain, dangling branches, and interactions with animals. Additionally, proceed with care while traversing riverbanks and bridges.

6. Adhere to safety signs and instructions
Along the Thames Path, pay heed to any warning signs, areas designated for walking, and advice from park rangers or local authorities on safety. Observe any

closures or limitations put in place to save delicate environments or guarantee public safety.

7. Maintain Communication

Keep a fully charged cell phone with emergency contacts preprogrammed, such as the non-emergency police number (call 101) and the local emergency services (dial 999). Give your schedule to a family member or trusted friend, and make sure they know where you are at all times by checking in with them.

Health Service of the Nation (NHS) For non-life-threatening medical crises, call 111.

The hotline for Thames River Watch is +44 (0)800 80 70 60. (To report pollution or occurrences along the river)

You may have a safe and enjoyable trip along the Thames Path, soaking in the history and beauty of England's famous river with peace of mind, by paying attention to these safety recommendations and being ready for any emergency. Take care of yourself, be safe, and enjoy every second of your Thames stroll experience.

Appendix

Useful Resources and Contacts

This appendix contains a list of helpful contacts and services to help you before, during, and after your trip down the Thames. These tools, which range from useful websites and instructive guides to crucial contact details for local authorities and emergency services, can improve your experience and provide invaluable support along the route.

1. The Thames Path National Trail website
The Thames Path website (www.nationalrail.co.uk)

Description: The Thames Path National Trail's official website offers a wealth of information for organizing your walk, including route maps, lodging alternatives, and updates on trail closures and conditions.

2. Guidebooks to the Thames Path
Publisher: A number of publishers
This category includes a variety of Thames Path reference books and maps that provide thorough route descriptions, historical context, and useful tips for hikers of all skill levels.

3. The Agency for Environment
The website for the Environment Agency is www.gov.uk/government/organisations.

Contact: 0345 988 1188 (for information and flood alarms), which is staffed around-the-clock.

The Thames Waterway Management Board, flood warnings, and river conditions are all covered by the Environment Agency.

4. TfL, or Transport for London
https://www.tfl.gov.uk

Customer service may be reached at 0343 222 1234.

Description: TfL provides information about London's public transport alternatives, such as riverboats that link to the Thames Path, buses, and trains.

5. Regional Travel Bureaus
Contact: A number of neighborhood travel agencies along the Thames

The Thames Path's towns and villages may provide information on local events, lodging options, and attractions via their local tourist offices.

6. Emergency Assistance
Emergency number to call is 999 (or 112).
Police Not-Urgent 101; National Health Service (NHS) - 111

Description: Dial 101 for non-emergency police help, 111 for NHS medical advice and assistance, and 999 (or

112) for emergency services in case of crises or urgent assistance.

7. Information Centers for Travelers
Contact: A number of the Thames Path's visitor centers Tourist information centers provide tourists with maps, brochures, and information on local services, lodgings, and attractions.

8. Internet Communities and Forums
Description: If you're looking to connect with other walkers along the Thames Path, ask questions, share experiences, and exchange stories, check our online walking, hiking, and travel groups.

9. Information about Accessibility
Description: Details on the amenities and features that make the Thames Path accessible, such as lodgings that are wheelchair-accessible and services for visitors with impairments.

10. Extra Materials
Additional resources that provide details on walking routes, outdoor activities, and attractions along the Thames include books, websites, and apps.

You will have access to useful information and help to improve your experience walking the Thames by making use of these resources and connections. Whether you're making travel plans, looking for local guidance, or need aid while out on your stroll, these tools will help guarantee a memorable, safe, and pleasurable experience along England's famous river.

CONCLUSION

Reflecting on Your Thames Journey

When your voyage down the Thames comes to a close, stop for a minute and consider the views, experiences, and memories you have gathered along the route. Walking the Thames is more than simply walking miles of beautiful routes; it's an opportunity to really engage with the rich history, vibrant culture, and breathtaking scenery that envelop this famous river in England.

You have followed the Thames's journey from its modest origins in the Cotswolds to its magnificent confluence with the sea. You have seen breathtaking vistas, quaint riverbank towns, and iconic sites that will never be forgotten as you travel the Thames Path.

You have seen historical colleges, opulent mansions, and classic architecture in historic places like Windsor and Oxford. You've strolled through peaceful meadows, verdant forests, and energetic market towns, stopping at each turn to see animals, breathtaking views, and undiscovered treasures.

You have marveled at the architectural feats of London's bridges, such as the recognizable Tower Bridge and the cutting-edge Thames Barrier, and you've felt the dynamic energy of the nation's capital as it flows alongside the banks of the rivers.

Most significantly, however, is that you've managed to establish a connection with the spirit of the Thames itself, a river that has fascinated and enchanted many travelers and artists for ages.

Remember that even after your footprints have faded from the route, the memories and experiences you have shared will remain with you when your Thames adventure comes to an end. You have set off on a voyage of exploration and adventure that will last a lifetime in your heart, regardless of how far you have strolled down the Thames or how little you have explored.

Take a minute to appreciate the river's beauty, the sun's warmth on your face, and the soothing sound of the water lapping against the beach as you say goodbye to the Thames. And never forget that the Thames is there to welcome you back whenever you're prepared to go off on another amazing voyage along its legendary waters.

May your trip down the Thames inspire and enhance your life, allowing the enchantment and wonder of England's most famous river to fill your days until we cross paths again.

Safe travels, fellow explorer

Continuing Your Exploration of England's Iconic River

As your trip along the Thames Path draws to a close, you may find it difficult to say goodbye to the captivating views and sounds of England's most famous river. Luckily, the last step of your stroll need not be the end of your tour of the Thames. Even after you've gone home, there are many options to extend your journey and strengthen your bond with this ancient river.

1. Examine Thames History and Culture in More Detail:

There are centuries' worth of untold tales in the Thames, a river rich in culture and history. Explore the rich history of the Thames via books, movies, and online resources. Learn about the river's significance in defining England's economic and cultural environment as well as its beginnings as a major trading route. Learn more about the river's importance and effects on the towns that have prospered along its banks for many years by visiting museums and historical sites along its course.

2. Investigate Uncharted Territory

The Thames Path provides a thorough path along the banks of the river, but there are plenty of undiscovered nooks and lesser-known sights that are just waiting to be discovered. Spend some time exploring off the main track to see remote riverbank towns, peaceful nature preserves, and obscure historical sites that provide a window into the Thames's more sedate and private side. If you want to see the river from a new angle, think about renting a kayak or paddleboard. You may even go on a guided boat trip to see secret locations and hidden jewels that are not accessible on foot.

3. Take in the Festivals & Events in Thames:
The Thames is home to several festivals, events, and festivities all year long that highlight both its natural beauty and cultural legacy. There's always something along the Thames that promises to amuse and inspire, from music festivals and modern art installations to historic regattas and riverbank markets. To learn about forthcoming events and chances to take in the river's majesty in novel and captivating ways, keep a watch on social media platforms and local event listings.

4. Encourage conservation and preservation efforts in the Thames
It's crucial to keep in mind the value of conservation and preservation efforts while you tour the Thames and take in its breathtaking beauty in order to save this priceless natural resource for future generations. Take into consideration joining neighborhood conservation groups or giving your time to habitat restoration and river cleanup initiatives. It is possible to guarantee that the Thames will continue to be a valued and popular travel destination for future generations by actively contributing to its health and vitality.

You are by no means done exploring England's most famous river as you consider your trip down the Thames and the memories you have created along the way. There are many chances to extend your experience and create a lasting relationship with the Thames for years to come, whether you want to support conservation initiatives, travel off the main route, attend riverfront events and festivals, or go deeper into its history and culture. Continue your journey of this ageless and well-loved river, keeping the spirit of adventure alive and exploring, discovering, and exploring.

Acknowledgement

It has been an amazing experience to write "Walking the Thames: A Guide to England's Iconic River," and I am appreciative of all the people and organizations who have helped make this project a reality.

First and foremost, I want to sincerely thank the English people for their unending inspiration, their love of the Thames River and their passion for sharing its history and beauty. This guide has been enhanced and elevated by their kindness, friendliness, and love for their country.

My sincere gratitude goes to the specialists, historians, and residents along the Thames who so kindly contributed their wisdom. Their knowledge and personal experiences have given this book a great deal of depth and authenticity, enabling readers to confidently and enthusiastically set off on their own Thames trip.

I owe a debt of gratitude to my friends and family for their consistent encouragement and support throughout the composition process. Their endurance, empathy, and confidence in me have been a continual source of support and inspiration, inspiring me to pursue greatness and conquer any obstacles in my path.

Finally, but just as importantly, I want to thank all of the readers of "Walking the Thames." We are honored that you have decided to go with our guide down England's most famous river. My genuine wish is that this book will be an invaluable tool for you, encouraging you to explore the Thames's treasures and make lifelong memories along its illustrious banks.

About the author

Monalisa Scott is more than simply a writer of travel guides; she is your ticket to fascinating and life-changing international adventures. With an ardent curiosity and an astute observation, Monalisa has devoted her professional life to enlightening people worldwide about her enthusiasm for travel and adventure.

Monalisa was born with a wanderlust that has carried her to many parts of the world, from thriving cities to secluded, beautiful settings. Her never-ending curiosity and need for new experiences have allowed her to find buried treasures, learn about local legends, and establish deep relationships with individuals from all over the globe.

In order to create thorough and perceptive travel guides that inspire and educate, Monalisa blends her own experience and knowledge with painstaking research. Monalisa's guides are your reliable travel companions, whether you're organizing a family holiday, a single backpacking excursion, or a romantic retreat. They provide helpful guidance, insider knowledge, and professional suggestions to ensure that your travels are as enjoyable as possible.

You may go off on an exciting and adventurous voyage with Monalisa Scott by your side, sure that you will be in capable hands the whole time. With Monalisa as your knowledgeable guide, prepare to travel the globe after packing your luggage and grabbing your guidebook. Awaiting you is your next amazing journey!

Printed in Great Britain
by Amazon

42211014R00059